LOVE and MARRI...

and DIVORCE

by Bob Zahn

CCC PUBLICATIONS

Published by

CCC Publications
9725 Lurline Avenue
Chatsworth, CA 91311

Manufactured in the United States of America

Cover ©1999 CCC Publications

Interior illustrations ©1999 CCC Publications

Cover/Interior art by Bob Zahn

Cover design by Bob Zahn

Cover production by Continental Imaging Center

ISBN: 1-57644-098-2

If your local U.S. bookstore is out of stock, copies of this book may be obtained by mailing check or money order for $6.99 per book (plus $2.75 to cover postage and handling) to:
CCC Publications; 9725 Lurline Avenue, Chatsworth, CA 91311

Pre-publication Edition – 8/99

Dedicated to Donna.
The love of my life.

Love and marriage and divorce! Love and marriage and divorce! Love and marriage and divorce! Keep doing it until you get it right.

Liz

'Tis better to have loved and lost than to never have loved at all, but this is getting ridiculous!

Zsa Zsa

"Listen, they're playing our song... no wait... that's Sally's and my song... or is it Brenda's and my song?..."

"I was an incurable romantic until I met
Frank the wonder drug!"

"Listen, Honey, they're playing our song."

"You'll always be number one with me,
Jim, but I've met number two."

"What do you mean our relationship isn't meaningful enough?
I've never seen you before in my life!"

"I'm sorry, Bill, but I've decided to downsize."

"Of course I love you for yourself, Ralph, you making two million dollars a year is just frosting on the cake."

"Actually, I was only looking for a one-night stand!"

"If it was your first date, maybe she just stood you up."

"You'd climb the highest mountain and swim the deepest ocean, but you won't co-sign a loan?"

"It's over for me, but he keeps hanging on."

"Yes, I remember you...I never forget a face or an idiot!"

"In my dream Prince Charming asked me to marry him!
I said no, but told him I would name a dog after him."

"I can't say yes or no right now, Steve, but
Vince's option runs out next month."

"It's nice to hear that you would die for me, Walter, but would you DIET for me?"

"If I marry you, is it alright for me to keep seeing Dave?"

"Why would I go out with a short, fat, bald guy like you?"
For one thing, you make me look good."

"I'm sorry, Fred, I'm very fond of you, but I prefer to remain footloose and fiancee free."

"It would never work, Leo, we come from
two different price ranges."

"I think George is getting serious. He took off his socks before we made love last night."

"You want me to marry you! Are you serious?"

"Does that mean you won't marry me?"

"...to love, honor and obey..."

"You look really beautiful in that gown...of course, I would too."

"I know you need your own space, Betty,
but separate honeymoons!"

"I'm glad we got that out of the way before
baseball season starts."

"For heaven sake, this is our HONEYMOON!"

"Carry mother in first."

"My husband is going to be really mad
if he finds out about this!"

"I'm going to go have a few drinks with the guys
...don't wait up for me."

"You may now pie the bride."

"Just put me on the couch and get me the TV remote."

"I promise I'll never call you immature again.
Now stop holding your breath!"

"My wife thinks I'm out fooling around
on her so I'm trying to oblige her."

"Of course my wife is frigid...isn't everybody's?"

"This isn't a marriage, it's a situation comedy!"

"I had a dream about you last night. Your
part was played by Tom Cruise."

"Of course I didn't marry Ralph for his money.
I married him for his father's money."

"One advantage of being married to Norma, when I want junk food, I don't have to go out for it."

"I don't want to get involved with a married man... not even my husband."

"You don't look miserable enough to be happily married."

"You're going to love it here! They give you
a day off every time you get married."

"You've started defending yourself lately, Ruby, don't you love me anymore?"

"Of course I remembered our anniversary.
Didn't you notice the moment of silence?"

"What do you mean I never take you anywhere?
I brought you here, didn't I?"

"My wife was busy, so I brought a friend."

and **DIV♥RCE**

"I've been happy and I've been married...happy is better."

"I tried marriage once. It was the longest three days of my life."

"You think that's stupid? Wait till you
hear what my ex-husband did..."

"I have to go to a wedding on saturday. I'm giving my ex-husband away."

"I didn't tell the kids that their father and I were getting divorced. I told them he was recalled because of defects."

"Actually, I know nothing about the meaning of life. The reason
I'm up here is because I'm hiding from my fourth wife!"

"I'm not walking out on you...I'm running!"

"...and these are my divorce pictures."

"It used to be Mom's Diner, but that's a long story."

"You're working too hard. My first husband
never used to come home too tired to argue!"

"I once thought I'd never find a husband and that was three husbands ago!"

"My ex-wife got half of everything in the divorce settlement and built her half into a fortune!"

"It's really disgusting the way you let that marriage
counselor push you around!"

"She's a housekeeper. Every time she gets divorced, she keeps the house."

"Sorry, but I'm going to have to let you go.
Both as an employee and a husband."

"Do you have any happy divorce anniversary cards?"

"Have my ex and I remained friends? We weren't friends when we were married!"

"The Complete Home Management System you bought
for the computer says I should divorce you."

"It's not the heat in the kitchen...It's the lack
of it in the bedroom!"

"We split everything four ways! My ex, me, and the two lawyers."

"I'm sorry, but it's strictly against my policy
to hire a former husband."

"She disappeared somewhere between the
World Series and the Super Bowl!"

"Messy divorce."

Thousands of Bob Zahn cartoons have been published in all the leading publications including Better Homes and Gardens, Woman's World, Playboy, First and countless other magazines worldwide. He has also had hundreds of greeting cards printed by many publishers including Marcel Schurman, Amberley, Freedom, Novo and several others. Love and Marriage and Divorce is Bob's sixth book.

TITLES BY CCC PUBLICATIONS

Blank Books ($3.99)
GUIDE TO SEX AFTER BABY
GUIDE TO SEX AFTER 30
GUIDE TO SEX AFTER 40
GUIDE TO SEX AFTER 50
GUIDE TO SEX AFTER MARRIAGE

Retail $4.95 – $4.99
"?" book
LAST DIET BOOK YOU'LL EVER NEED
CAN SEX IMPROVE YOUR GOLF?
THE COMPLETE BOOGER BOOK
FLYING FUNNIES
MARITAL BLISS & OXYMORONS
THE ADULT DOT-TO-DOT BOOK
THE DEFINITIVE FART BOOK
THE COMPLETE WIMP'S GUIDE TO SEX
THE CAT OWNER'S SHAPE UP MANUAL
THE OFFICE FROM HELL
FITNESS FANATICS
YOUNGER MEN ARE BETTER THAN RETIN-A
BUT OSSIFER, IT'S NOT MY FAULT
YOU KNOW YOU'RE AN OLD FART WHEN...
1001 WAYS TO PROCRASTINATE
HORMONES FROM HELL II
SHARING THE ROAD WITH IDIOTS
THE GREATEST ANSWERING MACHINE MESSAGES
WHAT DO WE DO NOW??
HOW TO TALK YOU WAY OUT OF A TRAFFIC TICKET
THE BOTTOM HALF
LIFE'S MOST EMBARRASSING MOMENTS
HOW TO ENTERTAIN PEOPLE YOU HATE
YOUR GUIDE TO CORPORATE SURVIVAL
NO HANG-UPS (Volumes I, II & III – $3.95 ea.)
TOTALLY OUTRAGEOUS BUMPER-SNICKERS ($2.95)

Retail $5.95
30 – DEAL WITH IT!
40 – DEAL WITH IT!
50 – DEAL WITH IT!
60 – DEAL WITH IT!
OVER THE HILL – DEAL WITH IT!
SLICK EXCUSES FOR STUPID SCREW-UPS
SINGLE WOMEN VS. MARRIED WOMEN
TAKE A WOMAN'S WORD FOR IT
SEXY CROSSWORD PUZZLES
SO, YOU'RE GETTING MARRIED
YOU KNOW HE'S A WOMANIZING SLIMEBALL WHEN...
GETTING OLD SUCKS
WHY GOD MAKES BALD GUYS
OH BABY!
PMS CRAZED: TOUCH ME AND I'LL KILL YOU!
WHY MEN ARE CLUELESS
THE BOOK OF WHITE TRASH
THE ART OF MOONING
GOLFAHOLICS
CRINKLED 'N' WRINKLED
SMART COMEBACKS FOR STUPID QUESTIONS
YIKES! IT'S ANOTHER BIRTHDAY
SEX IS A GAME
SEX AND YOUR STARS
SIGNS YOUR SEX LIFE IS DEAD
MALE BASHING: WOMEN'S FAVORITE PASTIME
THINGS YOU CAN DO WITH A USELESS MAN
MORE THINGS YOU CAN DO WITH A USELESS MAN
RETIREMENT: THE GET EVEN YEARS
LITTLE INSTRUCTION BOOK OF THE RICH & FAMOUS
WELCOME TO YOUR MIDLIFE CRISIS
GETTING EVEN WITH THE ANSWERING MACHINE
ARE YOU A SPORTS NUT?
MEN ARE PIGS / WOMEN ARE BITCHES
THE BETTER HALF
ARE WE DYSFUNCTIONAL YET?
TECHNOLOGY BYTES!
50 WAYS TO HUSTLE YOUR FRIENDS
HORMONES FROM HELL
HUSBANDS FROM HELL
KILLER BRAS & Other Hazards Of The 50's
IT'S BETTER TO BE OVER THE HILL THAN UNDER IT

HOW TO REALLY PARTY!!!
WORK SUCKS!
THE PEOPLE WATCHER'S FIELD GUIDE
THE ABSOLUTE LAST CHANCE DIET BOOK
THE UGLY TRUTH ABOUT MEN
NEVER A DULL CARD
THE LITTLE BOOK OF ROMANTIC LIES

Retail $6.95
EVERYTHING I KNOW I LEARNED FROM TRASH TALK TV
IN A PERFECT WORLD
I WISH I DIDN'T...
THE TOILET ZONE
SIGNS/TOO MUCH TIME W/CAT
LOVE & MARRIAGE & DIVORCE
CYBERGEEK IS CHIC
THE DIFFERENCE BETWEEN MEN AND WOMEN
GO TO HEALTH!
NOT TONIGHT, DEAR, I HAVE A COMPUTER!
THINGS YOU WILL NEVER HEAR THEM SAY
THE SENIOR CITIZENS'S SURVIVAL GUIDE
IT'S A MAD MAD MAD SPORTS WORLD
THE LITTLE BOOK OF CORPORATE LIES
RED HOT MONOGAMY
LOVE DAT CAT
HOW TO SURVIVE A JEWISH MOTHER

Retail $7.95
WHY MEN DON'T HAVE A CLUE
LADIES, START YOUR ENGINES!
ULI STEIN'S "ANIMAL LIFE"
ULI STEIN'S "I'VE GOT IT BUT IT'S JAMMED"
ULI STEIN'S "THAT SHOULD NEVER HAVE HAPPENED"

NO HANG-UPS – CASSETTES Retail $5.98
Vol. I: GENERAL MESSAGES (M or F)
Vol. II: BUSINESS MESSAGES (M or F)
Vol. III: 'R' RATED MESSAGES (M or F)
Vol. V: CELEBRI-TEASE